DR PHIL CUMMINS
CHARACTER EDUCATION SERIES

The Pathway to **Excellence**

The Pathway to **Excellence**

DR PHIL CUMMINS
CHARACTER EDUCATION SERIES

The Pathway to **Excellence**

BOOK 2

For the architects of my life.

Published in 2025 by Amba Press, Melbourne, Australia
www.ambapress.com.au

© Phil Cummins 2025

All rights reserved. No part of this book may be reproduced or transmitted in any form or by any means, electronic or mechanical, including photocopying, recording or by any information storage and retrieval system, without prior permission in writing from the publisher.

Cover design: Tess McCabe
Internal design: Amba Press
Editor: Rica Dearman

ISBN: 9781923215764 (pbk)
ISBN: 9781923215771 (ebk)

A catalogue record for this book is available from the National Library of Australia.

Contents

Foreword ix
Introduction: The Pathway to Excellence 1

Chapter 1
Learn 3
Values and beliefs 7
Personal development 12
Academic development 17
Step Forward and Up: Learn 22

Chapter 2
Live 25
Family and friends 29
Home life and finances 34
Relationship development 39
Step Forward and Up: Live 44

Chapter 3
Lead   47

Service and volunteering	51
Formal leadership	56
Leadership development	61
Step Forward and Up: Lead	66

Chapter 4
Work   69

Planning	73
Social purpose	78
Career development	83
Step Forward and Up: Work	88

Conclusion: Let's go!   91

Foreword

Hi! My name is Phil.

For more than thirty-five years, as an educator, researcher and speaker, I've been talking with and listening to hundreds of thousands of students, their families and teachers all over the world as they tell me what they want for their lives.

My mum, Rohma, has lived a long and meaningful life. She's the most strong-willed person I know and everything she does is characterised by a determination to keep going, keep learning and keep doing her best. What about you? What gets you up in the morning? What keeps you going? What drives your life? What makes you seek out excellence?

I think there are four ways you can grow in the character, competency and wellness throughout a life of being and becoming yourself:

1. **A Life of Purpose** – how to identify and claim the fundamental reason why for your journey of exploration, discovery and encounter.
2. **The Pathway to Excellence** – how to learn, live, lead and work as you strive to become the best version of yourself.
3. **Leading for Tomorrow's World** – how to connect your purpose to leadership which influences, inspires, directs and motivates others to build a shared vision for the future.

4. **Make a Difference** – how to create a plan to put your sense of purpose into practice for the sake of people and place and planet.

Drawing on the global research of three organisations that I lead (CIRCLE Education, a School for tomorrow. and the *Game Changers* podcast), I've written four books that explore in turn each of these four ways to grow in character. They're all about helping you to be well and grow in the knowledge, skills, dispositions and habits you need to understand what your purpose is and how you might learn, live, lead and work in pursuit of it.

This book, *The Pathway to Excellence*, is about becoming the best version of yourself. It teaches you how to ask and answer the powerful questions you need to learn, live, lead and work with success in our world.

So, what do you want for your life? What's important to you? What will help you to make your mark and measure up? Are you ready to take the big Step Forward and Up on **The Pathway to Excellence**?

Let's go!

Phil

Dr Phil Cummins FRSA FACEL FIML
Managing Partner, a School for tomorrow.
Managing Director, CIRCLE – The Centre for Innovation,
   Research, Creativity and Leadership in Education
Associate Professor of Education and Enterprise
Honorary Senior Fellow, University of Melbourne
Host, *Game Changers* podcast

Introduction
The Pathway to Excellence

Who am I? Where do I fit in? How can I best serve others? Whose am I?

These are the four questions that power **The Pathway to Excellence**, a journey to become the best version of yourself. This is an ongoing, inside-out process of being, becoming and transformation that can help you to both experience and contribute through a life of purpose. It's about helping you to grow, make progress, achieve and succeed.

Mastering the competencies to learn, live, lead and work that help to answer each of these four questions are ongoing challenges that speak to your formation as a person. A lot of this will be about the development of two qualities: self-efficacy (how you organise your character, competency and wellness to its best effect); and adaptive expertise (how you take this character, competency and wellness and use them to respond to the changing world around you).

With every step you take on **The Pathway to Excellence**, you are more likely to show the character, competency and wellness of which you are really capable. In doing so, you will increasingly feel a sense of belonging, achieve your potential, and do what is good and right in your life.

To follow **The Pathway to Excellence**, you will need to commit to a regular program of reflecting on who you have been, who you are and who you are becoming. This ongoing, inside-out process of self-awareness, relationship, selflessness and vocation can help you to learn, live, lead and work through a life of purpose. Throughout this book, I will be asking you to build a routine to help you to think about your growth as a person of character using a series of charts and reflective questions. I'll also share with you what I have learned from some of the guests on my podcast, *Game Changers*, about how to become the best version of yourself.

Are you ready to take your first step on **The Pathway to Excellence?**

Let's go!

Chapter 1
Learn

Learn

In the introduction, I introduced you to the competencies to learn, live, lead and work. In the next four chapters, we are going to dig deeper into each of these and their role on **The Pathway to Excellence**. Chapter 1, therefore, is all about the competency to learn.

Answering the question 'who am I?' is the gateway to building the competency to learn. Learning well helps you to become stronger in all the facets of your life and apply these strengths to realising an evolving and increasingly selfless reason for doing what you do. Learning, therefore, is about the quest towards self-awareness that fosters a sense of your purpose through a combination of both curiosity and wisdom so that you can meet the expectation to 'know yourself'.

By the end of this chapter, I am hoping you will be feeling increasingly confident about your ability to learn. You will be able to test this confidence against the following statements:

- I practise curiosity and wisdom.
- I seek to 'know myself'.
- I want to understand more about my values and beliefs, my personal growth and how to develop myself academically.
- I wrestle with the question 'who am I?'

- I am discovering more about what I stand for, what drives what I do in my life, and the character, competencies and wellness that I will need to make a positive difference.
- I am creating a stronger sense of who I might become and how I might bring benefit to others.

We will explore these three areas to help you discover how to grow in how and what you learn:

1. Values and beliefs
2. Personal development
3. Academic development

After working through each in turn, you will Step Forward and Up and begin to make a plan for how you will put into place what you are learning in this book.

Values and beliefs

What is good and right in your life? What are the best options for you? What choices will you make? How can you connect with a greater purpose?

How you do good and right in the world is as much about who you are and who you are becoming as it is about what you do. It is a continuing story of yesterday, today and tomorrow. This is a story that Lester Lalla, headmaster of St John's Preparatory School in Johannesburg, South Africa, understands well. He explained to me how he tries to tell a real story of himself, a story that intersects with that of the school he now leads:

I have to lead with a sense of authenticity who I am. I cannot put aside the parts of myself that are black, that are South African, that are cultural, that are filled with Ubuntu, which is an African word that encompasses one's humanity. I can't put those parts of myself aside. And so I've chosen to lead fully embracing who I am as a black male... It has not been easy, but it's been incredibly rewarding to just try and live out of my own authenticity.'

[From *Game Changers*: Series 14 Episode 1: Tradition Old & New – Lester Lalla, 13 June 2023, https://podcasts.apple.com/au/podcast/series-14-episode-1-tradition-old-new-lester-lalla/id1503430745?i=1000616716028]

In this section we will cover:

- Core beliefs and moral code
- Ethical decision-making
- Values in action
- Spiritual practice

When you're finished reading through each section, we'll take some time to reflect upon your values and beliefs, how you form them and how you live them out.

Core beliefs and moral code

Identifying and understanding your core beliefs and moral code is about how you come to know what is good and right in your life.

The chart below details how you can assess your ability to do this. On the left, you can see a set of **behaviours** and on the right, **indicators** of these behaviours. You can think of these **behaviours** as ways you act out your core beliefs and moral code. **Indicators** are statements that help you to understand these **behaviours** and work out whether you are currently doing them.

Read through this chart and think about how often you display the **behaviours** associated with identifying and understanding your core beliefs and moral code.

Core beliefs and moral code

Behaviour	Indicator	Rarely	Sometimes	Usually
Forming moral code	I have a set of beliefs that serves me well as an anchor for everything I do.			
Maintaining values	Even when things get tough, I would not knowingly or willingly violate or compromise my core beliefs.			
Exploring other beliefs	I am always seeking to explore and deepen my core beliefs through reading, reflection and discussion with others.			
Living with purpose	Living with purpose and integrity is very important to me.			
Benefitting others	Acting on my core beliefs or moral code improves the lives of others and is a source of good, not just personal gain.			

Ethical decision-making

Making choices based on ethical decision-making is about how you identify the correct options for you to live a life based on an appreciation of what is good and right according to your core beliefs and moral code.

Using the chart below, work out how often you make choices based on ethical decision-making.

Choices and ethical decision-making

Behaviour	Indicator	Rarely	Sometimes	Usually
Knowing right from wrong	I have a clear sense of what is the 'right' thing to do and can confidently apply this to the daily and sometimes difficult decisions I make.			
Maintaining academic integrity	I have a full understanding of what I need to do to meet all ethical standards for academic honesty and integrity in my studies.			
Making hard ethical choices	I am confident that I would choose to do the right thing even if doing so had negative consequences.			
Learning from mistakes	I have made mistakes in the past in my ethical judgement, but learning from these has made me better.			
Resisting temptation	I don't let pressure or circumstance override my sense of what's right and what's wrong to do.			

Values in action

Situating your values in action is to do with how you make specific choices about what you will and will not do according to the principles established in your core beliefs and moral code.

Read through the chart below and think about how consistently you are situating your values in action.

Situating values in action

Behaviour	Indicator	Rarely	Sometimes	Usually
Assessing own strengths	I can identify my best character strengths – those character skills and habits that contribute most to my success and wellbeing, and that I rely on most often and effectively.			
Adopting role models	I often see character strengths in others that I admire and wish I could have, too.			
Understanding character growth	I take the view that with focus and effort I can work on my character strengths and develop new ones, rather than seeing them as fixed and immutable.			
Supporting others' success	It is important to me that my character strengths contribute to the success and wellbeing of others, not just myself.			
Reflecting on character	I am becoming competent in reflecting on my 'character' and setting personal resolutions and goals for growth.			

Spiritual practice

Locating your actions in spiritual practice is about how you place what you value, believe and do within the context of something much greater than yourself, be that a sense of the divine, the way the world and the universe works and ought to work, or both, so long as this transcends your own self and asks you to contemplate a life spent in service of a higher purpose.

Use the **behaviours** and **indicators** below to reflect upon how you locate your code in your spiritual practice.

Locating actions in spiritual practice

Behaviour	Indicator	Rarely	Sometimes	Usually
Valuing spirituality	I appreciate the value of cultivating a personal spiritual perspective for my wellbeing and overall quality of life.			
Developing curiosity	I am very curious and interested in learning about different spiritual perspectives, traditions and practices.			
Being grateful and hopeful	I have a sense of gratitude and optimism that helps me put things in perspective and appreciate the world around me.			
Telling a spiritual story	If someone asked me, I could tell the story of my personal spiritual journey and the spiritual routines and practices that help me.			
Discussing spiritual matters	My friends and I enjoy discussing and debating our different spiritual perspectives, interests and practices.			

Personal development

Do you manage emotions well? Do you reflect on who you are, what you are doing, where you are going and who you are becoming? Do you live a healthy life? Do you feel well?

How you take the opportunities that are presented to you in life is central to answering questions such as these. Karen Mundine, CEO at Reconciliation Australia, is from the Bundjalung Nation of northern New South Wales. She has more than 25 years' experience leading community engagement, public advocacy, communications and social marketing campaigns. She spoke to me of the foundational role of her family in providing opportunities to her and her sisters and the continuing impact this has on her:

> *It really started with my grandparents. They wanted a better life for their growing family. They made a lot of sacrifices... so that their kids, my mum and her brothers and sisters, would have a better life, would have better opportunities for work. I think that was something that was drilled into me, and certainly our family, that we were given these opportunities of education, for different jobs, for different lives, for better lives. But part of that was that you had to give back, that you had to do something with this great opportunity that you were given.'*

[From *Game Changers*: Voice – Karen Mundine in Conversation with Phil Cummins Pt 1: Her Voice, 22 March 2023, https://podcasts.apple.com/au/podcast/voice-karen-mundine-in-conversation-with-phil-cummins/id1503430745?i=1000605215428]

In this section of the chapter, we will explore behaviours associated with:

- Emotional intelligence
- Reflective habits
- Health
- Wellness

Emotional intelligence

Building your emotional intelligence is about how you manage your own feelings and the feelings of others in your life.

Using the chart below, reflect on your progress in building your capacity to act with greater emotional intelligence.

Emotional intelligence

Behaviour	Indicator	Rarely	Sometimes	Usually
Emotional self-awareness	I am very self-aware of my emotional responses to things that are happening to me, and I am able to regulate my emotions.			
Describing own emotions	I am good at describing and talking about my emotions and thoughts with those whom I trust.			
Identifying others' needs	I am able to identify and understand the wants, needs and viewpoints of people around me.			
Collaborating with others	I work well with others, helping them to cooperate and collaborate in accomplishing a task or goal.			
Seeing things through	I am self-motivated and have the drive and perseverance to accomplish tasks and meet my goals.			

Reflective habits

Adopting a set of reflective habits is about how you routinely and constructively question what you are doing and who you are becoming.

Consider your current ability to reflect using this next chart.

Reflective habits

Behaviour	Indicator	Rarely	Sometimes	Usually
Stepping back	I am good at stepping away and assessing a situation, before making a decision about how to handle something.			
Showing perspective	I am able to put things in perspective and show gratitude for what I have and who I am, rather than getting worked up needlessly.			
Accepting criticism	I am able to take criticism and feedback in my stride and use it to help me build on my progress.			
Building a growth mindset	I bring a growth mindset to my thinking about my abilities and performance.			
Setting realistic goals	I am good at setting realistic personal goals for myself, figuring out the best ways to proceed and evaluating how well I am doing in meeting those goals.			

Health

Boosting your health is to do with how you make choices about what you will and will not do to become healthier physically and mentally in the short and long term.

Use the **indicators** below to consider how you display behaviours related to boosting your health.

Health

Behaviour	Indicator	Rarely	Sometimes	Usually
Accessing medical practitioners	I have access to a trusted doctor or other health practitioner for routine check-ups and as needed for professional help in addressing an illness or a health concern.			
Sleeping well	I have good sleep routines and am aware and knowledgeable about how much sleep I need to perform well.			
Managing substance usage	I keep myself informed about the health effects of substance use, monitor my behaviours, and make good and responsible choices for me.			
Eating and exercising well	I am informed about healthy living and make good choices about diet and exercise.			
Staying healthy sexually	I am knowledgeable about taking responsibility for my sexual health, making the right choices for me and always having respect for others.			

Learn

Wellness

Feeling well is often connected with your approach to how you learn, live, lead and work – the safe and supportive positive practices you do to stay well. While there are other factors to consider which will influence your wellness as a whole, one important thing you can do is to maintain a regime of doing what is right for you.

Use the chart below to determine how well you are using an appropriate and safe approach to maintaining your wellbeing.

Wellbeing				
Behaviour	Indicator	Rarely	Sometimes	Usually
Staying mentally healthy	I have the knowledge, skills and awareness to monitor my mental health and to recognise the signs of stress, anxiety, depression or self-harm.			
Resting and relaxing	I routinely find time to rest, enjoy myself and recharge.			
Reaching out to friends	I have good friends whom I would be comfortable reaching out to for support and help in dealing with a personal concern.			
Connecting with mentors	There is currently at least one older adult or professional in my life whom I would be comfortable talking to for advice about a personal concern or question.			
Seeking constructive help	Seeking help for a personal problem is to me a positive and good thing to do, not a sign of weakness or a source of shame.			

Academic development

Have you designed a program for your academic learning? Are you making progress with your academic goals? Do you want to do the work you need to do to improve academically? Are you gaining the qualifications you need?

As you go about the academic process, you need to be mindful that, at its heart, the outcome of your learning is always realised in its most fulfilling manner through the act of creation. Professor Michael Anderson from the University of Sydney is one of the world's leading experts on creativity in education and explained it to me like this:

We think creativity is an end in itself, but it is in many ways the gift that keeps on giving… To create is inevitably to give something of yourself, to make it public, to expose an inner part of who you are, to announce the world and to say, "I have something of value, I have something that's meaningful, I have something to contribute to the world."

[From *Game Changers*: Michael Anderson in Conversation with Phil Cummins Part 2: A Deeper Sense Of The World, 27 June 2024, https://podcasts.apple.com/au/podcast/michael-anderson-in-conversation-with-phil-cummins/id1503430745?i=1000660362053]

In this section we will cover:

- Academic program
- Academic progress
- Disposition towards study
- Academic grades and qualifications

Academic program

Building your academic program is about how you manage the process of entry and enrolment into a program of study and how you design it to match your best understanding of what you enjoy and what you are good at doing.

Use the chart below to reflect on your current progress in building your academic program.

Building an academic program

Behaviour	Indicator	Rarely	Sometimes	Usually
Researching career paths	I actively research what is required for the professions and career paths that interest me.			
Asking for academic advice	I have sought advice from many people I respect and trust in thinking about the focus of my educational planning.			
Anticipating change	I appreciate that my future career will take many twists and turns, and that I will need to engage in lifelong learning to flourish and be successful.			
Discovering academic options	I know how to research academic offerings that best build on my academic preparation and background, meet program requirements, and reflect my personal goals and ambitions for my education.			
Broadening an education	As much as it is possible to do so, I will make sure that I create opportunities for courses that enrich me and provide for a broader education.			

Academic progress

Establishing and maintaining your academic progress is about how you set goals and create personal habits that will result in a routine that is more likely to help you to meet course requirements and achieve the results that you deserve.

Read through the chart below and think about how you are establishing and maintaining your academic progress.

Establishing and maintaining academic progress

Behaviour	Indicator	Rarely	Sometimes	Usually
Setting learning goals	I set goals for my learning, progress and desired achievement in this course.			
Understanding course outcomes	I take every effort to ensure that I understand what the outcomes for the course are, how I will be evaluated and what skills I need to develop to be successful.			
Seeking clarification	If I am uncertain, I will seek clarification from my teacher about how I can improve in order to achieve my goals.			
Meeting educational responsibilities	I monitor how I am meeting my responsibilities as a student, to ensure that I am keeping up and on track for steady progress.			
Connecting with teachers	Whenever possible, I will get to know my teachers and be known and recognised, even though it is often difficult to achieve this.			

Disposition towards study

Strengthening your disposition towards study is about the choices you make about what you will and will not do to maintain a positive approach and take responsibility for your learning in your academic program.

Using the chart below, reflect on your ability to strengthen your disposition towards study.

Disposition towards study

Behaviour	Indicator	Rarely	Sometimes	Usually
Building study habits	I have effective study habits that work for me, and I am constantly evaluating how well they help me succeed in my courses, making adjustments as necessary.			
Relating well with classmates	I realise that I need others in my class to help me succeed and to learn well, and I take care to develop good relationships with my classmates.			
Being open-minded with learning	I bring the habits of open-mindedness, curiosity and wonder to my courses.			
Asking for help	When I have a problem or challenge, I will ask my teacher for guidance on how to solve the problem myself.			
Expanding a perspective	I take advantage of the opportunities to learn from different perspectives and to think deeply about the topics in my courses.			

Academic grades and qualifications

Understanding academic grades and qualifications helps you to place what you are learning and what you need to achieve in your academic program within the context of what you will need to maximise your choices later in your life.

Read through the chart below and determine how well you understand academic grades and qualifications.

Academic grades and qualifications

Behaviour	Indicator	Rarely	Sometimes	Usually
Recording academic qualifications	I keep a personal log of my academic records and any qualifications gained over my learning career.			
Researching academic qualifications	I research and understand the qualifications for various professions and careers, and monitor whether I am on track to acquire those qualifications.			
Seeking advice on qualifications	I seek the advice of professionals in the fields that interest me to ensure that my qualifications pathway meets my needs.			
Reflecting on growth through courses	At the end of each course, I take stock of my experience and achievement, and reflect on how I have grown in knowledge and exercised competency and mastery.			
Refining a learning program	I reset my learning goals and refine my academic program to support my progress on my academic journey.			

Step Forward and Up

Learn

I believe that to learn what really matters in life on **The Pathway to Excellence**, it's important for you to develop your self-awareness and identity. During this chapter, we examined three key areas that can help you to do this:

- ✓ Values and beliefs
- ✓ Personal development
- ✓ Academic development

I am hoping now that you might be able to identify with the following statements from the beginning of this chapter with greater confidence:

- I practise curiosity and wisdom.
- I seek to 'know myself'.
- I want to understand more about my values and beliefs, my personal growth and how to develop myself academically.
- I wrestle with the question 'who am I?'
- I am discovering more about what I stand for, what drives what I do in my life, and the character, competencies and wellness that I will need to make a positive difference.
- I am creating a stronger sense of who I might become and how I might bring benefit to others.

Which of these makes the most sense to you right now? How might you grow even stronger in it? Which statement do you find most challenging? How might you overcome this challenge?

What's next in developing the competency to **Learn** for you?

Think about how your thinking about this and personal development might work together. When you are ready, let's start Chapter 2, so we can explore the second competency: to live.

Let's go!

Chapter 2
Live

Live

In this chapter, we will explore what it means to live well on **The Pathway to Excellence**.

Answering the question 'where do I fit in?' is a great starting point to growing in the competency to live. Living well helps you to understand and respect yourself and others, and the language, customs, honourable traditions, rituals and values of the people and places from which you have come and to where you are going. Living, therefore, is the search for relationship that helps you to appreciate your people and your place with the humility and gratitude that helps you to meet the expectation to 'earn your place'.

By the end of this chapter, I am hoping you will be more certain about what it takes to live well. You will be able to test this confidence against the following statements:

- I practise gratitude and humility.
- I seek to 'earn my place'.
- I want to understand more about my family and friends, my home life and finances, and how to develop my relationships.
- I wrestle with the question 'where do I fit in?'
- I am discovering more about the language, customs, honourable traditions and culture that help me to bring honour to my people and care for my place.

- I am creating a deeper understanding about the importance of fellowship with my family, friends, colleagues and community, and respect for my home.

Let's consider three key areas to help you discover how to grow in how you might live well:

1. Family and friends
2. Home life and finances
3. Relationship development

We'll work through each in turn, then continue to build your plan to Step Forward and Up.

Family and friends

Are you grateful for your family? Are your friendship groups positive and constructive? Are you engaged in social activities and clubs that enable you to grow, connect with and serve others? Are you broadening your life through sports and the arts?

I think that it's important to think through how you balance your commitments to yourself and to your family and friends. I really admire how my friend Benjamin Cooper, who is a very successful executive chef at Chin Chin, as well as a thinker and writer, maintains his focus on what really matters to him:

 My career is a never-ending source of energy and joy from which I get to draw to complete the other component of my life, which is even more important: my family – my wife and my kids mean the world to me. I don't know if everyone gets to experience a complete circle of life and purpose, but mine, the two components of what really makes me happy, are harmoniously linked.'

[From *Game Changers*: Series 17 Episode 189 Benjamin Cooper (Part 1): Without Fear, 24 September 2024, https://podcasts.apple.com/au/podcast/series-17-episode-189-benjamin-cooper-part-1-without-fear/id1503430745?i=1000670457345]

In this section we will cover:

- Family connections
- Friendship groups
- Social activities and clubs
- Sports, the arts and other activities

Family connections

Building healthy family connections that last is about how you come to know, appreciate and show lifelong gratitude for the positive and practical gifts that relationships with family can and do bring to them and to you.

Using the chart below, reflect on your current capacity to build healthy family connections that last.

Healthy family connections

Behaviour	Indicator	Rarely	Sometimes	Usually
Reaching out to family	I always reach out to family members to find out how they are doing, what they might need and how I might help them.			
Valuing extended family	I consider my extended family as rich in experience and wisdom that I can learn from.			
Appreciating family support	I express my gratitude to my family for the care and support which has taken me to my current stage.			
Considering family advice	I am respectful of and give thoughtful consideration to the advice of my family in shaping my educational and career journey.			
Working through family relationship challenges	I don't run away from problems with close family members but instead try to find ways of repairing the relationship.			

Not all of us have families or are in a position to connect with our families on an ongoing basis. If you are in this situation, please feel free to use this chart to talk about the group of people who act as a family for you or else just move on to the next section.

Friendship groups

Establishing and maintaining constructive friendship groups is to do with how you go about identifying and caring for friends who bring to your relationships the values, beliefs and structure that create an environment of trust and reciprocity in which all might grow to fulfil their potential and to do what is good and right in their lives.

Reflect on the indicators and behaviours below to think through how you establish and maintain constructive friendship groups.

Constructive friendship groups

Behaviour	Indicator	Rarely	Sometimes	Usually
Discussing life with my friends	I enjoy chatting and arguing with my friends about how best to live and what it means to flourish.			
Establishing my trusted friend	I have at least one good friend whom I know would be there for me if I needed help of any sort.			
Seeking different acquaintances	I go out of my way to be friendly with people who aren't 'just like me' and who help me to see the world from different perspectives.			
Making friends	I work on making new friends while keeping old ones.			
Supporting friends	I am someone my friends can count on if they need someone to talk to about a difficult personal issue.			

Social activities and clubs

Balancing social activities and clubs is about how you select which groups of people you will join that will align with and support your lifestyle and sense of belonging, the fulfilment of your potential and your propensity to do that which is good and right.

Reflect on the chart below and consider how well you are developing a range of social activities that will enhance your sense of connectedness and increase your important relationships.

Social activities and clubs

Behaviour	Indicator	Rarely	Sometimes	Usually
Keeping social	I recognise that social activities are good for my mental health and my general wellbeing, and I pursue them actively.			
Being a responsible member	When I am attending events or participating in club activities, I take responsibility for myself and show care for others.			
Being a well-regarded member	Others consider me to be a positive member of any activity I join, and someone they could trust to bring good judgement to any situation.			
Volunteering for community service	Each year, I volunteer for a service or community agency, project or initiative that makes a positive difference in the lives of others.			
Encouraging diverse participation	I encourage a diverse range of people and friends to join in the activities which I enjoy and value.			

Sports, the arts and other activities

Improving your involvement in sports, the arts and other activities is about how you develop your recreational interests with other people in your life within the context of the time that is available to you and what you enjoy.

Use the chart below to reflect on how your involvement in sports, the arts and other activities contributes to your recreational life.

Sports, the arts and other activities

Behaviour	Indicator	Rarely	Sometimes	Usually
Committing to activities	Each year, I make or renew a significant commitment to one or two teams, groups or activities.			
Trying new activities	I will try out new sports or cultural activities to see if they interest me and would meet my needs.			
Practising my skills	As a member of a team or group, I take pride in practising and developing my skills.			
Valuing teammates	I value greatly the friendships I make in my activities, and the personal network I build.			
Cheering on others' efforts and success	I admire what others with different talents and passions do and take an interest in their success and achievement.			

Home life and finances

Do you know how to contribute to creating the right home for you and those you care for? Do you have or are you aiming to find a job that provides appropriately for you and aligns with your sense of purpose? Do you know how to manage your money? Do you know how to organise and manage your time well?

The way you build a sense of home has a great bearing on your capacity to pursue your goals. How you manage money is critical in this. Lacey Filipich founded Money School as a social enterprise to help young people think about developing the habits that can lay down a foundation for a life of financial security. She explained what she has learned about the relationship between who you are and how you live:

 I think it comes down to personal character, both that belief about yourself and some things that might be hardwired in us… I think that personal dedication is required to recognise what's important to you and then build accordingly.'

[From *Game Changers*: Series 7 Episode 1: Money School – Lacey Filipich, 20 July 2021, https://podcasts.apple.com/au/podcast/series-7-episode-1-money-school-lacey-filipich/id1503430745?i=1000529417786]

In this section we will cover:

- Building a sense of home
- Employment and earning capacity
- Finances and personal debt
- Calendar and time management

Building a sense of home

Building a sense of 'home' for yourself and for those with whom you live is about how you select a safe and potentially happy place in which you can establish the lifestyle, routines and physical appearance that will give you a sense of belonging.

Look through the chart below and reflect on how you could build a sense of 'home' for you and your loved ones.

A sense of 'home'

Behaviour	Indicator	Rarely	Sometimes	Usually
Assessing shared accommodation	Before living with others in shared accommodation, I would be careful to assess whether the arrangement would be right for my personality and goals.			
Checking legal responsibilities for accommodation	I am aware of the legal rights and obligations when renting accommodation and always check that I am fully protected before agreeing to anything.			
Checking accommodation for safety	In choosing an area or building to live in, my personal safety and wellbeing are prime considerations.			
Being a good neighbour	I am considerate of my neighbours and those around me, and strive to be a good member of the community in which I live.			
Keeping house	I do my fair share of the chores and take care that my living conditions are healthy and conducive to my studies.			

You may still be living with your parents and have not yet needed to find accommodation for yourself, so you might like to think about how you might answer these questions for when you need to do so.

Employment and earning capacity

Establishing and maintaining your employment and earning capacity is to do with how you go about qualifying for and finding meaningful employment that will support your chosen lifestyle in a way that is both morally and ethically in accordance with your values and beliefs.

Think through how you might establish and maintain your employment and earning capacity using the chart below.

Employment and earning capacity

Behaviour	Indicator	Rarely	Sometimes	Usually
Knowing what matters	I reflect deeply on what matters most to me and how my employment and earning capacity might relate to this.			
Researching income	I research and have a good sense of the income/salary profile and range of jobs and professions that might interest me.			
Planning for student debt	In my planning to acquire higher qualifications for my career or profession, I am aware of the student debt I will most likely incur along the way.			
Consulting financial advisors	I seek the advice of experts and people I trust in making good choices about my future career in light of my personal and financial goals.			
Anticipating change	I know that my career pathway will have many twists and turns, and that I will need to learn and unlearn continuously in order to achieve my personal and financial goals.			

The sooner you start to think and become knowledgeable about the issues associated with your employment and earning, the better prepared you will be to take responsibility for what will be a very important source of both stability and stress at different stages of your life.

Finances and personal debt

Managing your finances and personal debt is to do with how you make specific choices about what level of personal debt you will and will not take on to support the lifestyle that you choose to lead.

Think through what you know about how to manage your finances and personal debt using the chart below.

Finances and personal debt

Behaviour	Indicator	Rarely	Sometimes	Usually
Understanding educational costs	I thoroughly research what it's going to cost to support my education, including tuition, school expenses and living costs.			
Tracking daily expenses	I use apps or other methods to keep track of my expenses and income on a daily basis.			
Establishing a savings plan	I set aside enough money each month to put into a savings account, knowing that this can make a difference.			
Controlling expenses	I exercise good self-discipline in controlling my expenses, to ensure that I am in good financial shape.			
Understanding personal credit	I know the consequences of not being able to pay my bills for my financial security and my credit rating.			

Calendar and time management

Managing your calendar and time is about how you place what you are doing and achieving in your life within the context of the time that is available to you and your choices about how best to spend it.

Look through the list of **behaviours** and **indicators** below to consider your current ability to manage your calendar and time.

Calendar and time management

Behaviour	Indicator	Rarely	Sometimes	Usually
Using a daily calendar	I keep and update a calendar to organise, schedule and meet my commitments.			
Meeting daily tasks and long-term goals	I accomplish what I need to each day, ensuring that I meet important goals for my personal life and education.			
Reviewing weekly schedules	At the end each week, I review how things went during the previous week and what I should prioritise and accomplish in the week ahead.			
Establishing strong personal routines	I have good study, work and rest habits, and strive to improve them.			
Exercise and relaxation	Each day I take time to both relax and exercise.			

Relationship development

How well do you connect with other people? How well do you listen and speak? How well do you understand, fit into and shape the culture of those around you? How well are you valued by those around you?

Dr Briony Scott has led schools and represented educators at the highest level in Australia. She has been recognised for her leadership, achievements and personal impact. She identified to me the essential quality of appreciating 'the other' in relationship development:

Gratitude never goes one way. It's always around recognising what other people have done to enable you to do your job and then recognising that you also enable people or you disable them to be able to do their job. So, it's a very symbiotic kind of relationship.'

[From *Game Changers*: Lead Through Who You Are – Briony Scott in Conversation with Phil Cummins Part 2: Learning To Grow, 15 September 2022, https://podcasts.apple.com/au/podcast/lead-through-who-you-are-briony-scott-in-conversation/id1503430745?i=1000579539838]

In this section we will explore:

- Relational skills
- Language skills
- Cultural fit and understanding
- Perceived belonging and social standing

Relational skills

Improving your relational skills is about how you develop your ability to listen with care and empathy to the voice of others and to seek out ways to find common ground, appreciate difference, resolve conflict and achieve the satisfaction of mutual interests and concerns.

Look through the chart below and think about what you are currently doing to build a robust and resilient sense of your belonging and social standing.

Relational skills

Behaviour	Indicator	Rarely	Sometimes	Usually
Reflecting on relationality	I reflect on my relational skills, becoming aware of what I need to do to be effective in my relationships with others.			
Maintaining trust	I strive to be trustworthy, responsible and collegial in my relationships with others.			
Exercising empathy	I am empathetic and know how to put other people at ease.			
Easing tensions	When tensions or difficulties arise, I do my part to help diffuse the situation, resolve the conflict and get everyone back on track.			
Seeking relational advice	I ask those whom I respect and admire what they consider to be the important relational skills for success.			

Language skills

Developing your language skills is about how you deepen your understanding of how to communicate with other people.

Use the chart below to think through your willingness to learn a language other than your own so that you can improve the richness, depth and compassion of your own and others' experience of the world.

Language skills

Behaviour	Indicator	Rarely	Sometimes	Usually
Planning improved language skills	I have a plan to improve my language skills, being clear about how best to progress in my learning.			
Gaining second language fluency	I've set myself a high standard to become fluent in a second language over the course of my education.			
Seeking feedback on language skills	I do my best and am prepared to make mistakes in order to get feedback as to how I can get better with my use of language.			
Extending second language skills	I use multiple means to develop my second language skills, including reading, social media, formal study, my work and friends.			
Practising language skills daily	I work hard every day to improve my communication skills in my first and second language.			

Cultural fit and understanding

Improving your cultural fit and understanding is about how you identify with and respond to the history, culture and honourable traditions of your social grouping while also connecting with and learning from those of other communities.

Use the chart below to think about how you currently relate to the background of others by adopting an open and respectful approach to cultural fit and understanding.

Cultural fit and understanding

Behaviour	Indicator	Rarely	Sometimes	Usually
Building intercultural awareness	I am interested in expanding my knowledge about the history, values, beliefs and behaviours of cultures and ethnic groups other than my own.			
Valuing diverse environments	I appreciate that working effectively with individuals from diverse groups and with different viewpoints is a critical skill for my learning and work.			
Interacting with different work colleagues	I embrace opportunities to interact with others who are different from me, and I enjoy the experiences that come up.			
Developing intercultural skills	Even when it feels difficult to continue, I persevere in developing my intercultural skills and perspective.			
Evaluating intercultural skills	I am able to evaluate how well I am progressing in developing my intercultural skills and setting new goals for my development.			

Perceived belonging and social standing

Building a sense of perceived belonging and social standing is about how you recognise that you are connected to, bring value to, gain from and are valued by your network of family and friends for the contributions and humanity you bring to others.

Use the chart below to think through how you are building a sense of perceived belonging and social standing at present.

Perceived belonging and social standing

Behaviour	Indicator	Rarely	Sometimes	Usually
Aspiring to contribute	I aim to make a real contribution to the world around me.			
Energising self through purpose	I am motivated and invigorated by my sense of purpose and direction.			
Energising self through others' aspirations	I seek the company, acknowledgement and support of friends, classmates and others who want to accomplish great things.			
Sourcing inspiration through role model achievements	I am inspired by the example of role models and outstanding people in any field or interest who achieve their purpose and make a positive difference.			
Securing mentors to support purpose and direction	I have trusted people in my life who are there to help me discover my purpose and direction and find my voice.			

Step Forward and Up
Live

I believe that to live with meaning on **The Pathway to Excellence**, you need to develop your purpose through growing in connection and relationship. In this chapter, we explored three areas that can help you to strengthen the competency to live:

- ✓ Family and friends
- ✓ Home life and finances
- ✓ Relationship development

Let's use the same process to consolidate your understanding of each of these as we did in Chapter 1. Consider each of the following statements from the start of this chapter:

- I practise gratitude and humility.
- I seek to 'earn my place'.
- I want to understand more about my family and friends, my home life and finances, and how to develop my relationships.
- I wrestle with the question 'where do I fit in?'
- I am discovering more about the language, customs, honourable traditions and culture that help me to bring honour to my people and care for my place.
- I am creating a deeper understanding about the importance of fellowship with my family, friends, colleagues and community, and respect for my home.

Which of these makes the most sense to you right now? How might you grow even stronger in it? Which statement do you find most challenging? How might you overcome this challenge?

What's next in developing the competency to **Live** for you?

When you are ready, let's start Chapter 3, so we can explore the third competency: to lead.

Let's go!

Chapter 3
Lead

Lead

All of us lead others at some point in our lives. Whether we lead on a large scale or by setting an example, we are all responsible for how we shape the lives of others. In this chapter, we will make a start on how we can accept this responsibility to lead on **The Pathway to Excellence**.

Asking the question 'how can I best serve others' is an excellent prompt to help you to gain more of the competency to lead. Leading well begins with who you are, flows into who you want to become and is demonstrated through intentional action with the means to influence, inspire, direct and motivate others to achieve a preferred future for all. Leading, therefore, is about the challenge of selflessness that helps you to locate your practice with the courage and compassion necessary to meet the expectation to 'go on a journey from me to you to us'.

By the end of this chapter, I am hoping you will be more certain about what it takes to lead well. You will be able to test this confidence against these statements:

- I practise courage and compassion.
- I seek to 'go on a journey from me to you to us'.

- I want to understand more about service and volunteering, formal leadership experience and how to develop my leadership.
- I wrestle with the question 'how can I best serve others?'
- I am discovering more about how to direct, motivate, influence and inspire others to achieve a preferred future for us all.
- I am creating a clearer picture of a shared vision for our future, and deliberate and intentional ways for us to get there together.

We will explore these three areas to discover more about your leadership:

1. Service and volunteering
2. Formal leadership
3. Leadership development

Let's work through each in turn, then Step Forward and Up together.

Service and volunteering

Do you offer and give support to your family regularly? Do you set the right example and help your friends? Do you volunteer your service in your social clubs and activities? Do you lead in your sporting, artistic and other pursuits?

Much of the habit, instinct and will to serve is innate to us. Our circumstances will help to bring out aspects of this through our lives, but all of us have the capacity to give to others and make a difference in their lives. Ronni Kahn AO, the founder of the food rescue charity OzHarvest and Australian Local Hero of the Year in 2010, put it like this:

 People look at me today and think they couldn't possibly do anything out of the ordinary or they couldn't possibly become leaders. I think every single one of us is a leader. Some of us have titles, some of us don't, but every single one of us is a leader.'

[From *Game Changers*: Series 10 Episode 1: Social Impact With Heart – Ronni Kahn, 25 May 2022, https://podcasts.apple.com/au/podcast/series-10-episode-1-social-impact-with-heart-ronni-kahn/id1503430745?i=1000563666493]

In this section we will cover:

- Service to family
- Service in friendship groups
- Service in social activities and clubs
- Service in sports, the arts and other activities

Service to family

Building healthy habits of service to your family is about how you respond to the kinship in helping them by offering your time, energy and commitment to their progress and wellness.

Read through the chart below and think about how you currently build healthy habits of contribution to your family.

Service to family

Behaviour	Indicator	Rarely	Sometimes	Usually
Supporting family	I reach out to other family members, to find out how they are doing, what they might need and how I might help them.			
Easing family tensions	I help others in my extended family to get along and gain some perspective on things when there is conflict or tension.			
Balancing family expectations	I strike what is for me the right balance between my obligation and service to my family and my own ambition and goals.			
Valuing family sense of mission	I think a family should have a shared mission and sense of purpose, and I am willing to advance it.			
Contributing to a family service project	I would contribute my time and leadership to a service or volunteer project that my family would sponsor and run.			

Service in friendship groups

Establishing constructive service in friendship groups is to do with how you go about serving your friends and acquaintances through the example you set and the positive and active leadership you provide in the right context.

Use the chart below to reflect on how you currently establish and maintain a constructive presence in your friendship groups.

Service in friendship groups

Behaviour	Indicator	Rarely	Sometimes	Usually
Providing support to friends	My friends can count on me to offer support, and to watch out for everyone's safety and wellbeing.			
Including newcomers in friendship groups	My friends and I will invite outsiders to join in our activities.			
Using social media positively	I use social media in a way that does not demean, harm or isolate others and I will stand up if I see that happening.			
Volunteering with friends	My friends and I often volunteer together to support an activity or project that helps others.			
Maintaining diverse friendship groups	My friendship groups are diverse and I enjoy that feature of them.			

Service in social activities and clubs

Providing service in social activities and clubs is about how you manage volunteering your time and other resources to support the ongoing viability and activities of the clubs and social communities to which you belong.

Look through the chart below and think about how you provide service in social activities and clubs.

Service in social activities and clubs				
Behaviour	Indicator	Rarely	Sometimes	Usually
Participation in service projects	I am currently involved in service projects or initiatives through my school or community agencies.			
Following significant philanthropists	I admire and follow those philanthropists who identify a big problem or challenge and leverage significant change and betterment.			
Supporting administrators	I have recently helped manage or run a club activity.			
Supporting inclusivity	When I am involved in a social or club activity, I try to make sure that it is inclusive and respectful of everyone.			
Volunteering willingly	I am a willing and helpful volunteer when I hear the call to contribute to make something successful.			

Service in sports, the arts and other activities

Contributing service in sports, the arts and other activities is about how you contribute service and leadership to your significant pastimes within the context of the time that is available to you and what you enjoy.

Reflect upon how you are currently contributing service in your sports, the arts and other activities.

Service in sports, the arts and other activities

Behaviour	Indicator	Rarely	Sometimes	Usually
Identifying barriers to group cohesion	If team or group cohesion is not going well, I will help name the problem and address it constructively.			
Helping team members who struggle	I reach out to teammates or members of an activity who seem to be having a hard time.			
Speaking up for others	I am always prepared to speak up if I think someone is being demeaned or harassed.			
Valuing team ethos	The values and ethos of the team or activity are just as important to me as its success.			
Valuing team service initiatives	I believe that every team should have a service initiative or project attached to it and I am willing to contribute to this.			

Formal leadership

Are you a leader in your setting? How do you provide leadership in your community? Do you understand how to bring out the best in people so that they can do what they need to, to do better? How well do you reflect on and plan for improvement in your leadership?

Leadership is the art of influencing, inspiring, directing and motivating people so that they work together to achieve the goals of the team or the broader organisation. Understanding your motivation to lead is critical. In 2006, siblings Rosie and Lucy Thomas founded Project Rockit, an anti-bullying campaign that would grow into a national youth-driven movement for positive social change. They recognised that there was an opportunity to improve the situation of young people whose lives were being adversely affected by the negative behaviour of others. They were mindful of the powerful reason why they wanted to lead and how they wanted to go about this. Rosie explained this as follows:

The biggest motivator for starting this organisation was more wanting to make a difference, wanting to engineer a better world… We wanted to put the issues back in the hands of young people, give them the tools and the skills to be able to create the change that they want to see in the world.'

[From *Game Changers*: Series 5 Episode 6: Embedding Kindness – Rosie & Lucy Thomas, 30 March 2021, https://podcasts.apple.com/au/podcast/series-5-episode-6-embedding-kindness-rosie-lucy-thomas/id1503430745?i=1000514948627]

In this section we will cover:
- Formal leadership planning and reflection
- Formal leadership in a community context
- Formal leadership in an educational context
- Formal leadership in a work context

Formal leadership planning and reflection

Improving your formal leadership planning and reflection habits is about how you reflect on your capacity to evaluate your leadership and the potential for your growth through different leadership experiences.

Read through the chart below and think about your habits of planning and reflection for your formal leadership.

Planning and reflecting on formal leadership

Behaviour	Indicator	Rarely	Sometimes	Usually
Planning formal leadership development	I have a clear but flexible plan for my formal leadership development that spans my responsibilities and aspirations across a variety of settings.			
Reflecting on own leadership quality	I reflect constantly on the quality of my work as a leader, using a variety of sources of feedback and information to help me improve.			
Establishing a reliable leadership track record	Consistency and quality of commitment, reliability, initiative and self-discipline are fundamental to my reputation in all the settings in which I contribute and lead.			
Aligning leadership to purpose	I take a holistic and integrated perspective on my leadership in many settings, centred by my sense of purpose, integrity and the values that matter most to me.			
Developing leadership competency	In my leadership development planning, I ensure that I am developing my perspective and competencies as a future-fit leader.			

Formal leadership in a community context

Experiencing leadership in a community context is to do with how you go about serving your friends and acquaintances in the broader community through the formal leadership you provide to them in different organisations and groups.

Look through the chart below and think about how you engage with leadership in a community context.

Experiencing leadership in a community

Behaviour	Indicator	Rarely	Sometimes	Usually
Being informed about volunteering opportunities	I keep myself informed about formal opportunities for volunteer leadership positions in organisations that have a service or advocacy purpose.			
Taking responsibility for thriving communities	I believe that all of us have a responsibility to help our communities flourish and their members thrive.			
Aspiring to formal leadership	I aspire in time to hold formal leadership roles in organisations that help others and improve the community.			
Contributing to community activities	I engage in a variety of community activities as opportunities to make a contribution, to learn about service and community building, and to develop my leadership skills.			
Committing to innovation projects	I would like to contribute my time, knowledge and skills to the creation of innovative and enterprising solutions in the community and service sector.			

Formal leadership in an educational context

Many reading this book will be at school or in further study of some form. Experiencing leadership in an educational context is about how you manage taking up formal leadership opportunities while undergoing formal education and balancing the responsibilities that arise from both.

Using the chart below, reflect on how you engage with leadership in an educational context.

Experiencing leadership in a school or educational community

Behaviour	Indicator	Rarely	Sometimes	Usually
Being informed about leadership opportunities	I keep myself informed and interested in formal opportunities for leadership positions at my current school, university or program.			
Seeking advice about leadership from leaders	I find opportunities to interact with senior leaders, instructors and administrators in relation to my personal leadership developmental plan and goals.			
Showing initiative	In any role I take on, I show commitment and initiative, and make a significant contribution.			
Setting and reflecting on activity goals	Small or large, I set some personal goals for the activity, and reflect on what I have learned and grown in when the activity concludes.			
Taking stewardship in learning communities	I feel an obligation to be a responsible steward of the learning communities and institutions that I am associated with.			

Formal leadership in a work context

Many reading this book will also have a job. Experiencing leadership in a work context is to do with how you go about providing service and leadership to employers, colleagues and associates within an employment setting.

Read through the chart below and think about how your **behaviours** currently align with experiencing leadership in a work context.

Experiencing leadership in a workplace

Behaviour	Indicator	Rarely	Sometimes	Usually
Being informed about work opportunities	I keep myself informed and interested in internships, contracts and salaried positions that afford me opportunities to further develop my knowledge and skills as a leader, to apply these fully to the benefit of others, and to be impactful.			
Discussing own leadership skills with supervisors	Discussing opportunities to test and develop my leadership skills is an important topic in my meetings with my supervisors or directors.			
Seeking guidance of mentors	Whether employed by an organisation or self-employed, I seek the guidance of a personal mentor or coach who can help me reflect on my leadership skills and work on improvement.			
Leading for innovation	I strive to take on roles where I can use my skills in problem-solving and creative thinking in leading others to generate innovative products, services and solutions.			
Modelling adaptive expertise and self-efficacy	I try to model resilience and a growth mindset in the face of change and to organise and use my character and competencies to the best of my ability within the culture of the organisation.			

Leadership development

Leadership development is a learning process by which each of us can build the character, competency and wellness to take responsibility for our community. We need to understand that this is best done as a deliberate and intentional process.

Jeanette Cheah is the founder and CEO of HEX, an award-winning edtech company that delivers internationally recognised programs to university students and the next generation of talent. She explained her motivation in promoting the ongoing development of the character of leaders throughout all levels of society who are both innovators and contributors through the exercise of their capabilities:

I believe if you don't have a centre and you're not doing things authentically and have an obligation to people, planet, society, community, that you're not actually innovating in a way that's going to help the world.'

[From *Game Changers*: Series 11 Episode 2: Uplifting Leadership – Jeanette Cheah, 9 August 2022, https://podcasts.apple.com/au/podcast/series-11-episode-2-uplifting-leadership-jeanette-cheah/id1503430745?i=1000575448002]

In this section we will cover:

- Leadership development program
- Leadership development progress
- Disposition towards leadership
- Leadership qualifications

Leadership development program

Building your leadership development program is about how you manage your process of enrolment or entry into a program of leadership development, and how you design it to match your best understanding about what you enjoy and what you are good at doing.

Using the chart below, think through how you are building your leadership development program.

Leadership development program

Behaviour	Indicator	Rarely	Sometimes	Usually
Including leadership development in planning	My leadership development is an important component in my educational planning and progress.			
Researching leadership development	I research and identify courses and programs offered at my school or university and by agencies or associations in planning for my personal leadership development.			
Seeking leadership development advice	I seek advice from others in planning my personal leadership development program.			
Broadening leadership learning	I look for opportunities to broaden my understanding of leadership through a diverse range of subjects and disciplines.			
Connecting leadership theory and practice	I build connections between the leadership courses and programs I undertake and my practical leadership experiences.			

Leadership development progress

Maintaining your leadership development progress is about how you set goals and create personal habits that will result in a routine that is more likely to help you to meet program requirements and achieve the results that you deserve.

Using the chart below, reflect upon your leadership development progress and how you are maintaining it.

Leadership development progress

Behaviour	Indicator	Rarely	Sometimes	Usually
Setting leadership development goals	Each year I set goals for my progress in developing leadership skills.			
Meeting with leadership development mentors	It is important that I meet at least once annually with a mentor to review my progress in my leadership development plan.			
Meeting with leadership development teachers	I take advantage of opportunities to meet with my teachers and instructors to talk about my goals for and interest in my leadership development.			
Refining leadership learning plan	I modify and adjust my personal leadership development plan to take into account my progress to date.			
Staying up to date with thought leadership	I keep up with the best and most innovative thinking on the purpose, practice and competencies of future-fit leadership, and hone my leadership development plans accordingly.			

Disposition towards leadership

Boosting your disposition towards leadership is to do with how you make specific choices about what you will and will not do to maintain a positive approach towards taking responsibility for your learning in your leadership development program.

Use the chart below to think about how you are working to boost your disposition towards leadership.

Disposition towards leadership

Behaviour	Indicator	Rarely	Sometimes	Usually
Self-belief in learning capacity	I believe that leadership is not something innate but rather a competency that can be learned over time.			
Expertise in leadership	I am strongly motivated to becoming a leader who has a wide array of relevant knowledge, skills and dispositions.			
Servant leadership	I am passionate about becoming a servant leader who helps others to thrive and contribute their best effort to the work at hand.			
Deepening sense of purpose	I find and value the time to reflect on and deepen my sense of purpose at the heart of my leadership.			
Learning from others	I take full advantage of the opportunities to reflect on and learn from the different leadership perspectives and styles I observe and witness around me.			

Leadership qualifications

Attaining leadership qualifications is about how you demonstrate that what you are learning and achieving in your leadership development program qualifies you to be considered for positions of formal and informal leadership. Although a qualification indicates a willingness to continue learning and apply yourself to the task, it does not automatically prove readiness or capacity for leadership.

Use the chart below to think about your current approach to attaining leadership qualifications.

Leadership qualifications

Behaviour	Indicator	Rarely	Sometimes	Usually
Recording leadership qualifications and experience	I keep an ongoing log of my academic credits, qualifications and experiences in my leadership development.			
Recommendations, references and referees	I routinely seek out my instructors, employers, directors and coaches for letters of recommendation and support for my leadership development portfolio.			
Taking advice	I seek the advice of experts to ensure that my success in achieving my leadership development plan is optimal and beneficial.			
Adaptive expertise in leadership	I reflect on how I have grown in knowledge and mastery in developing my leadership competency.			
Leadership journey	I can articulate and communicate my journey as a leader, using my personal log and portfolio to document and enrich my story.			

Step Forward and Up

Lead

I believe that to live with genuine impact on **The Pathway to Excellence**, you need to develop your purpose through growing in service and contribution. Throughout Chapter 3, we reviewed three areas in this competency to lead:

- ✓ Service and volunteering
- ✓ Formal leadership
- ✓ Leadership development

We will use the process you should know well by now to review your progress and Step Forward and Up. There is a reason we use the same set of questions – the more we use a known structure to guide our behaviours, the more likely we will develop a positive habit that will help to ingrain these behaviours so that they become a trusted routine. The routines we adopt (so long as we remain conscious and purposeful about what they are, why we are doing them and when they are relevant to our circumstances) mean that we can walk **The Pathway to Excellence** with a growing sense of expertise and accomplishment.

Please consider each of the statements identified at the start of the chapter:

- I practise courage and compassion.
- I seek to 'go on a journey from me to you to us'.
- I want to understand more about service and volunteering, formal leadership experience and how to develop my leadership.

- I wrestle with the question 'how can I best serve others?'
- I am discovering more about how to direct, motivate, influence and inspire others to achieve a preferred future for us all.
- I am creating a clearer picture of a shared vision for our future, and deliberate and intentional ways for us to get there together.

Which of these statements makes the most sense to you right now? How might you grow even stronger in it? Which statement do you find most challenging? How might you overcome this challenge?

What's next in developing the competency to **Lead** for you?

When you are ready, let's start Chapter 4, so we can explore the fourth and final competency: to work.

Let's go!

Chapter 4
Work

Work

In this chapter, we will consider the fourth competency on **The Pathway to Excellence**: work.

Work is part of who we are and how we are built as human beings. All of us need to apply our thoughts, emotions and physical efforts towards a set of tasks that get a job done. Some jobs we like, some we don't, but there is a sense that jobs are something we have to do. These jobs, and how we approach them, therefore, can be very important in how we achieve our purpose in life.

Answering the question 'whose am I?' tells us much about how we can connect purpose with our work. Working well often comes from building a supportive network of people and place for and with whom your sense of belonging, the achievement of your potential and the propensity to do that which is good and right in your life – your character – might all find a meaningful home. Working, therefore, is about the discovery of commitment that helps you to connect your purpose, your people and your place within your practice through the vocation and diligence required to meet the expectation to 'find your calling'.

By the end of this chapter, I want you to be able to say the following with assuredness:

- I practise commitment and diligence.
- I seek to 'find my calling'.

- I want to understand more about planning, social purpose and my career development.
- I wrestle with the question 'whose am I?'
- I am discovering more about what might be a purpose for my efforts, my contributions and my resources that goes well beyond myself.
- I am creating a network of people around me who help each other feel as though they belong and can fulfil their potential while they do what is good and right in the world.

With these statements in mind, there are three key areas I suggest you explore to discover more about how to work well:

1. Planning
2. Social purpose
3. Career development

Work through each, then Step Forward and Up at the end of the chapter.

Planning

Do you set goals for yourself? Do you take responsibility for your life and follow through with your commitment? Can you manage a project well? How effective are you at evaluating yourself and your performance?

As we go about our planning, it's important to allow ourselves (and those we work with) a combination of both process and freedom. We all need some structure to help us be accountable to ourselves and others for what we do. Yet we can't become too rigid. Nicole Dyson, the founder of Future Anything, explains the importance of this in her own life as she contemplated how to transition from being a classroom teacher into founding her own enterprise based on teaching young people the knowledge, skills, dispositions and habits of entrepreneurship:

I need to be able to do something different. And I think all great stories start with like permission. And in this moment, I was lucky to have a leader who stepped back and had enough faith in me, and gave me the flexibility and the freedom to play.'

[From *Game Changers*: Finding Your Way – Nicole Dyson in Conversation with Phil Cummins Part 3: Engaged and Ready, 19 August 2021, https://podcasts.apple.com/au/podcast/finding-your-way-nicole-dyson-in-conversation-with/id1503430745?i=1000532440854]

In this section we will cover:

- Goal setting
- Self-regulation
- Project management
- Evaluation and assessment skills

Goal setting

Developing your propensity towards goal setting is about how you create meaningful plans to define what you want to achieve in your life.

Using the chart below, think through your current propensity towards goal setting and how you could be strengthening it.

Career goals

Behaviour	Indicator	Rarely	Sometimes	Usually
Valuing competency	I know that I need to practise and develop core future-fit competencies in order to thrive along my career journey.			
Researching career interests	I know where and how to research sources that give me knowledge about and insight into the career areas that interest me.			
Connecting to others for career advice	I know how to find and connect to those who can help me evaluate and make good decisions about my career interests, pathway and goals.			
Thinking flexibly about careers	In my career planning, I avoid rigid thinking, knowing that I may need to adjust and adapt to changing circumstances and opportunities.			
Career and purpose	My thinking and planning are grounded in my sense of purpose that informs the numerous choices that will comprise my career journey.			

Self-regulation

Identifying and understanding the consistency of your self-regulation is about how well you take responsibility for and follow through with organising yourself and your life.

Look at the chart below and think about the consistency of your self-regulation.

Self-regulation

Behaviour	Indicator	Rarely	Sometimes	Usually
Framing setbacks as opportunity	I have the resiliency to overcome setbacks and to frame mistakes as opportunities to learn better.			
Developing self-efficacy	I am developing my sense of efficacy as I develop my goals, pursue my ambitions, and learn how to adapt to change and uncertainty.			
Meeting new situations	I have good time management and work habits, and continue to improve these to meet new expectations, standards and challenges.			
Deferring reward	I am prepared to make sacrifices in order to gain success and achieve my career goals.			
Response to adversity	I control my reactions to difficulties, tensions and disagreement with others and find ways to strengthen productive collaboration.			

Project management

Improving your skills in project management is about how you make specific choices to construct plans and achieve your goals in a timely and resource-effective fashion.

Consider your skills in project management and what you are doing to improve them using the chart below.

Project management				
Behaviour	Indicator	Rarely	Sometimes	Usually
Organisational vision	I am able to relate the vision of the organisation to the work at hand and help those around me understand and be energised.			
Positive attitude	I bring open-mindedness and the ability to adapt to new information, uncertainty and change to current and future projects.			
Moving around obstacles	I help my team resolve issues that hinder progress, tap into everyone's knowledge and ideas, and achieve the desired goals.			
Data-based solutions	I am good at designing systems and pathways for information gathering, decision-making, implementation and evaluation.			
Team decision-making	I help the team drive towards the most creative and innovative decisions, solutions and results.			

Evaluation and assessment skills

Developing evaluation and assessment skills is about how you use both evidence and intuition to make sound judgements about the degree of success you are having in accomplishing your plans.

Think about your current evaluation and assessment skills and how you can develop them, referencing the chart below.

Evaluation and assessment skills

Behaviour	Indicator	Rarely	Sometimes	Usually
Reflecting on process	I am constantly reflecting on my goal-setting processes to ensure I am on the right path and using the right tools.			
Evaluating situations	I bring good evaluative reasoning to decisions and actions, assessing whether conclusions and judgements are evidence-informed, soundly determined and appropriate.			
Assessing own skills	I am good at assessing my personal and interpersonal skills, finding out what I need to learn to be better in my work and career development.			
Transferring skills	I identify and work on the transferrable skills that would enhance my position and help me expand my repertoire of competencies for my career development.			
Welcoming feedback	I welcome the input and advice of others to help me improve my performance.			

Social purpose

Have you earned a good reputation and a way of reinforcing it through a personal brand? Can you connect your purpose with your people and your place, and realise it through your practice? Do you build your social standing honourably? Are you having the right impact on the world around you?

Each of us needs a purpose in life that is higher than ourselves: how we might give of ourselves for the benefit of others. Benson Saulo is a remarkable Australian. Born to an Aboriginal mother and Papua New Guinean father, he is a proud descendant of the Wemba Wemba and Gunditjmara Aboriginal nations of Victoria, and of the New Ireland Province of Papua New Guinea. He's had a varied career as an activist, financier, diplomat and politician. He brings a unique perspective to how to think about finding a sense of direction for his social purpose.

I've chosen my path, and the best advice that I can offer other people is to strive for unity rather than uniformity, noting that there's not just one way of effecting change. We need to be able to form an understanding or common ground of what we're ultimately trying to achieve and working towards that together.'

[From *Game Changers*: What's Really Important – Benson Saulo in Conversation with Phil Cummins Part 2: Managing Complexity, 1 December 2020, https://podcasts.apple.com/au/podcast/whats-really-important-benson-saulo-in-conversation/id1503430745?i=1000500886511]

In this section we will cover:

- Personal branding
- Purpose, place, people, practice
- Social recognition
- Social impact

Personal branding

Adopting an ethical approach towards personal branding is about how you can build a reputation for doing what is good and right according to your core beliefs and moral code.

Refer to the chart below and think about your approach towards personal branding.

Personal branding

Behaviour	Indicator	Rarely	Sometimes	Usually
Live the values	Integrity and the values I uphold are core to my person and career; they can be seen clearly in how I work.			
High quality	I set a high standard for the quality and professionalism of my work.			
Making good decisions	I am a sound and timely decision-maker who uses information wisely, consults effectively and thinks creatively.			
Clear communication	I communicate clearly and effectively and am able to explain complex issues and solutions.			
Selflessness	I try to be a genuine servant of my community.			

Purpose, place, people and practice

Identifying and understanding your purpose, place, people and practice is about how you align your way of life with your values to create vocation.

Think about the **behaviours** and **indicators** in the chart below. Although most of this will develop throughout your career, consider your understanding of your purpose, place, people and practice at this stage.

Purpose, place, people, practice

Behaviour	Indicator	Rarely	Sometimes	Usually
Establishing personal purpose	I can explain my purpose and show how it is aligned with the mission of the organisation in which I work.			
Connecting purpose to place	My purpose responds to the place where I work – the culture, ethos, relationships and ways by which results are achieved.			
Linking people to purpose	My purpose is in service of the progress, success and wellness of the people with whom I work.			
Guiding practice with purpose	My purpose guides my practice – how I act to meet my responsibilities to ensure that the organisation achieves its goals.			
Purpose and planet	I refine, deepen and strengthen the relationship of my purpose to the world over the course of my career journey.			

Social recognition

Gaining appropriate social recognition is about how you make specific choices that will build your standing in your community.

Use the chart below to ask yourself what your current capacity to gain appropriate social recognition is.

Social recognition

Behaviour	Indicator	Rarely	Sometimes	Usually
Personal integrity	My values and my capacity to put them into action with honesty, decency and truthfulness are held in high regard.			
Excellent reputation	The reputation of the team, group or organisation and regard for its achievements are important to me.			
High standards	I would like to be remembered as someone who held myself to the highest standard for the quality of my work and contribution.			
Respectful relationships	I am consistently regarded as someone who exercises and models respectful interpersonal relationships.			
Positive contribution	Others would judge my work as worthy, accomplished and impactful.			

Social impact

Locating vocation through your social impact is about how you set and achieve goals that will bring benefit to the lives of others in accordance with your sense of social purpose.

Use the chart below to reflect on how well you locate vocation through your social impact.

Vocation and social impact

Behaviour	Indicator	Rarely	Sometimes	Usually
Sound solutions	My work motivates others to tackle challenges and come up with sound decisions and innovative solutions.			
Benefits for others	My work brings tangible benefits to those with whom I work and also the wider community.			
Organisational support	My personal sense of purpose supports the mission of the organisations with which I am associated.			
Dedicated service	I put my talents, knowledge and skills generously towards the service of others.			
Belonging and inclusion	My work and career advance belonging and inclusion in my organisation and community.			

Career development

Do you have a program to develop your career? Are you making progress with it? Do you have a sense of your vocation and a commitment to making it happen? Have you built a solid profile or work experience and internships?

As you contemplate how you will build your career, it's important to think about how you feel about this. For some, the future is a scary thing. Yet, what I've learned from people like Helen Connolly is that how you think and feel about what lies ahead makes a big difference to how you take on the challenge of tomorrow's world. Helen is the Children's Commissioner for South Australia. She's held positions as a social worker and a public servant, raised a family, travelled and contributed significantly to how Australia sees the rights of children. She told me about her approach to maintaining her optimism:

There was this really big adventure, risk taking, striving for something better and the future being very positive. The future was always portrayed to me as something good, something positive and something that was exciting. And I think that's the kind of thing that really sits with you.'

[From *Game Changers*: The Voice of a Child – Helen Connolly in Conversation with Phil Cummins Part 1: Learn From Others, 24 March 2022, https://podcasts.apple.com/au/podcast/the-voice-of-a-child-helen-connolly-in/id1503430745?i=1000555055479]

In this section we will cover:

- Career development program
- Career development progress
- Disposition towards career
- Work experience and internships

Career development program

Building your career development program is about how you manage your process of entry into a specific program of career development, and how you design it to match what you enjoy and what you are good at doing.

Use the chart below to think through how you're building your career development program.

Career development program

Behaviour	Indicator	Rarely	Sometimes	Usually
Career and education pathways	I know how to investigate options for my desired career pathway and for the design for my educational and career development.			
Professional services support	I know how to make use of professional career services in designing my educational and career pathway.			
Course and program qualifications	My program choices ensure that I will accumulate appropriate qualifications.			
Personal interest	My program choices make it possible for me to pursue personal interests that will deepen my sense of purpose and my career objectives.			
Course competencies	I map out how my choices of courses, programs and activities build my acquisition of future-fit competencies.			

Career development progress

Establishing and maintaining your career development progress is about how you set and achieve goals in your career so you can grow in your character, competencies and wellness, while also attending to the practical requirements of looking after yourself and those who share your life.

Use the chart below to think about establishing and maintaining your career development progress.

Career development progress

Behaviour	Indicator	Rarely	Sometimes	Usually
Career growth	I begin each year by reflecting on my career development strategy and determine my specific goals for the upcoming year.			
Career narrative	I reflect on and share the 'narrative' of my career development journey, including my sense of purpose, ambition, current strategies, choices and decision points.			
Personal network	I cultivate a personal network with people accomplished in the career fields that interest me, in order to make better decisions about the educational and career choices in front of me.			
Recording career qualifications and experiences	I keep a record of the qualifications, accreditations and other valuable information that forms a record of my career development program.			
Reviewing career development	I periodically review all aspects of my career development pathway, including my academic and professional courses and program requirements, my growth in future-fit competencies and my ways to gain hands-on work experiences.			

Disposition towards career

Your disposition towards a career is to do with how you make specific choices about what you will and will not do to build a career that enables you to attain a sense of belonging, achieve your potential and do what is good and right within the fields of your choice.

Reflect on your disposition towards your career and how you can boost it, referring to the chart below.

Disposition towards career

Behaviour	Indicator	Rarely	Sometimes	Usually
Aligning career to purpose	I seek to develop a career journey that I find fulfilling and that affirms my sense of purpose.			
Working through change	I know that I may well change my career many times, and that it is the purpose-driven journey that matters.			
Taking on professional learning	I know that I need to be adaptable and engage in lifelong learning in order to upgrade my knowledge and develop my competencies.			
Developing competencies progressively	I have a growth mindset in terms of developing my skills and competencies to meet new challenges and acquire new knowledge.			
Positive momentum	While I know that it will involve both ups and downs, I am optimistic about my career development and pathway.			

Work experience and internships

Developing your career through work experience and internships is about how you make the most of the opportunities presented to you for work within the context of what you will need to maximise your choices now and later in your life.

Complete a review of the chart below on work experience and internships.

Work experience and internships

Behaviour	Indicator	Rarely	Sometimes	Usually
Choosing work strategically	I am intentional and strategic in identifying work experiences and internships that provide me with new learning opportunities for my career path and development.			
Finding opportunities	I am active in finding opportunities to undertake a variety of tasks, and I establish good working relationships with leaders whom I consult for career guidance and insight.			
Being reliable	I have a reputation for commitment, reliability, punctuality, effort and achievement and for my effectiveness.			
Going beyond the role	I offer to take on extra tasks that give me the opportunity to demonstrate my skills.			
Reviewing work experience	At the end of my work experience or internship, I ask for a meeting with my supervisor to review my work and career development pathway and to extend my personal network.			

Step Forward and Up

Work

I believe that to work towards a lifetime of progress and success on **The Pathway to Excellence**, you need to develop your purpose through growing in vocation and enterprise. We discussed three areas in this competency to work during this chapter:

- ✓ Planning
- ✓ Social purpose
- ✓ Career development

Let's Step Forward and Up with these. Please reflect on each of the statements I put to you at the start of the chapter:

- I practise commitment and diligence.
- I seek to 'find my calling'.
- I want to understand more about planning, social purpose and my career development.
- I wrestle with the question 'whose am I?'
- I am discovering more about what might be a purpose for my efforts, my contributions and my resources that goes well beyond myself.
- I am creating a network of people around me who help each other feel as though they belong and can fulfil their potential while they do what is good and right in the world.

Which of these statements makes the most sense to you right now? How might you grow even stronger in it? Which statement do you find most challenging? How might you overcome this challenge?

What's next in developing the competency to **Work** for you?

Once you have resolved this, let's conclude with the final stage of **The Pathway to Excellence**.

Let's go!

Conclusion
Let's go!

In this second book of the **Character Education Series**, we have made great progress in helping you to become the best version of yourself.

In travelling together on **The Pathway to Excellence**, I've shared with you what I've learned about how to learn, live, lead and work as you strive to become the best version of yourself.

I've also invited you to Step Forward and Up in each chapter by thinking through some questions and identifying some of the things that you can use to put into action your sense of what each of the elements of **The Pathway to Excellence** mean to you.

If you have found what we have done together to be valuable, there are two further books in this series that you might like to consider:

- **Leading for Tomorrow's World** – how to connect your purpose to leadership which influences, inspires, directs and motivates others to build a shared vision for the future.
- **Make a Difference** – how to create a plan to put your sense of purpose into practice for the sake of people and place and planet.

If you haven't already, you might also find value in reading the first book in the series:

- **A Life of Purpose** – how to identify and claim the fundamental reason why for your journey of exploration, discovery and encounter.

Before we finish, there's one final thought I'd like to share with you.

Our world is a pretty difficult place. Navigating your way forward within it can be complicated, especially when you're not sure that you're really doing what matters and doing it well. Some things endure while others move fast, and it isn't always clear what our practice should be. The stories of the *Game Changers* I have included in this book point to a way forward to writing your own playbook.

The journey of **The Pathway to Excellence** has the potential to help you to unlock your humanity because it draws on the qualities of curiosity, compassion, courage and conviction to connect you to a sense of something greater than yourself. You will likely always wrestle with the needs of your inner self and the demands and expectations of the outer world, and might never quite resolve the two. But you will do the work of building the civic character of belonging, the performance character of fulfilling your potential and the moral character of doing what is good and right. After all, if you let what is outside of you drive what is inside of you, you are far more likely to claim a purpose that will allow you to go the distance.

No one ever has *the* answer, but we must keep thinking about and contributing our own ideas about what might be a better way to help those around us thrive in their world. Hope and faith are so important in this.

We need to be measured and rational in how we judge what matters, what works and what should be done. There needs to be a balance in what we might seek that allows us to choose carefully what we keep, what we try and (most importantly) what we discard.

When we know what really matters to us, and we can align this intention, this purpose to our practice, then we will be in a much better position to measure our progress towards becoming better versions of ourselves.

That's the promise of **The Pathway to Excellence**: a journey of exploration, discovery and encounter.

After all, life is an adventure.

Let's go!

www.ingramcontent.com/pod-product-compliance
Lightning Source LLC
Chambersburg PA
CBHW050303120526
44590CB00016B/2473